The Hemophiliac's Motorcycle

The Hemophiliac's

Motorcycle

POEMS BY TOM ANDREWS

University of Iowa Press Ψ Iowa City

University of Iowa Press, Iowa City 52242

Copyright © 1994 by Tom Andrews

All rights reserved

Printed in the United States of America

Design by Richard Hendel

http://www.uiowa.edu/~uipress

Printed on acid-free paper

Library of Congress Cataloging-in-Publication Data

Andrews, Tom, 1961–

The hemophiliac's motorcycle: poems / by Tom Andrews.

p.   cm.—(Iowa poetry prize)

ISBN 0-87745-452-3

I. Title.   II. Series.

PS3551.N4537H46   1994

811´.54—dc20   93-43994

03   02   01   00   99   P   5   4   3

FOR CARRIE

Contents

• • • • • •

Acknowledgments

• • • • • •

The poems in this book originally appeared (a few in earlier versions or under different titles) in the following publications, to whose editors grateful acknowledgment is made: *Antioch Review*: "Evening Song"; *Field*: "The Hemophiliac's Motorcycle" and "Codeine Diary"; *Poetry*: "Praying with George Herbert in Late Winter" and "Reading the Tao Te Ching in the Hospital," copyright © 1992 Modern Poetry Association; *Virginia Quarterly Review*: "Hymning the Kanawha"; *Westminster Review*: "When Comfort Arrives"; *Witness*: "At Burt Lake," "Ars Poetica," "A Visit to the Cathedral," and "Reading Frank O'Hara in the Hospital."

"When Comfort Arrives" and "Hymning the Kanawha" also appeared in *Hymning the Kanawha*, a limited-edition chapbook published by Haw River Books, Ltd. "At Burt Lake" and "Ars Poetica" also appeared in *The Art and Craft of Poetry* by Michael J. Bugeja (Cincinnati: Writer's Digest Books, 1994). "Hymning the Kanawha" also appeared in *A While Longer before the Cold: An Anthology*, edited by Jack Ridl (Holland, Mich.: Hope College, 1990). "Evening Song" was also printed as a broadside at Twinrocker Mill in Brookston, Indiana.

My thanks to Mike Chitwood, Tony Crunk, and Charles Wright for their help with the body of the text and to Andrew Van Slooten, M.D., and Emily Worden-Meuleman, R.N., M.S.N., for their help with the text of the body.

i
· · · · · ·

The Hemophiliac's Motorcycle

. . . . . .

For the sin against the HOLY GHOST is INGRATITUDE.
—Christopher Smart, *Jubilate Agno*

May the Lord Jesus Christ bless the hemophiliac's motorcycle, the smell of knobby tires,

Bel-Ray oil mixed with gasoline, new brake and clutch cables and handlebar grips,

the whole bike smothered in WD40 (to prevent rust, and to make the bike shine),

may He divine that the complex smell that simplified my life was performing the work of the spirit,

a window into the net of gems, linkages below and behind the given material world,

my little corner of the world's danger and sweet risk, a hemophiliac dicing on motocross tracks

in Pennsylvania and Ohio and West Virginia each Sunday from April through November,

the raceway names to my mind then a perfect sensual music, Hidden Hills, Rocky Fork, Mt. Morris, Salt Creek,

and the tracks themselves part of that music, the double jumps and off-camber turns, whoop-de-doos and fifth gear downhills,

and me with my jersey proclaiming my awkward faith—"Powered By Christ," it said above a silk-screened picture of a rider in a radical cross-up,

the bike flying sideways off a jump like a ramp, the rider leaning his
whole body into a left-hand corner—

may He find His name glorified in such places and smells,

and in the people, Mike Bias, Charles Godby, Tracy Woods, David and
Tommy Hill, Bill Schultz—

their names and faces snowing down to me now as I look upward to
the past—

friends who taught me to look at the world luminously in front of
my eyes,

to find for myself the right rhythm of wildness and precision, when
to hold back and when to let go,

each of them with a style, a thumbprint, a way of tilting the bike this
way or that out of a berm shot, or braking heavily into a corner,

may He hear a listening to the sure song of His will in those years,

for they flooded me with gratitude that His informing breath was
breathed into me,

gratitude that His silence was the silence of all things, His presence
palpable everywhere in His absence,

gratitude that the sun flashed on the Kanawha River, making it
shimmer and wink,

gratitude that the river twisted like a wrist in its socket of
bottomland, its water part of our speech

as my brother and I drifted in inner tubes fishing the Great
    White Carp,

gratitude that plump squirrels tight-walked telephone lines and
    trellises of honeysuckle vines

and swallows dove and banked through the limbs of sycamore trees,
    word-perfect and sun-stunned

in the middle of the afternoon, my infusion of factor VIII sucked in
    and my brother's dialysis sucked in and out—

both of us bewildered by the body's deep swells and currents and
    eerie backwaters,

our eyes widening at the white bursts on the mountain ash, at
    earthworms inching into oil-rainbowed roads—

gratitude that the oak tops on the high hills beyond the lawns
    fingered the denim sky

as cicadas drilled a shrill voice into the roadside sumac
    and peppergrass,

gratitude that after a rain catbirds crowded the damp air, bees
    spiraling from one exploding blossom to another,

gratitude that at night the star clusters were like nun buoys moored
    to a second sky, where God made room for us all,

may He adore each moment alive in the whirring world,

as now sitting up in this hospital bed brings a bright gladness for the
  human body, membrane of web and dew

I want to hymn and abide by, splendor of tissue, splendor of cartilage
  and bone,

splendor of the taillike spine's desire to stretch as it fills with blood

after a mundane backward plunge on an iced sidewalk in Ann Arbor,

splendor of fibrinogen and cryoprecipitate, loosening the blood
  pooled in the stiffened joints

so I can sit up oh sit up in radiance, like speech after eight weeks
  of silence,

and listen for Him in the blood-rush and clairvoyance of the
  healing body,

in the sweet impersonal luck that keeps me now

from bleeding into the kidney or liver, or further into the spine,

listen for Him in the sound of my wife and my father weeping
  and rejoicing,

listen as my mother kneels down on the tiled floor like Christopher
  Smart

praying with strangers on a cobbled London street, kneels here in
  broad daylight

singing a "glorious hosanna from the den"

as nurses and orderlies and patients rolling their IV stands behind
them like luggage

stall and stare into the room and smile finally and shuffle off, having
heard God's great goodness lifted up

on my mother's tongue, each face transformed for a moment by
ridicule

or sympathy before disappearing into the shunt-light of the hallway,

listen for Him in the snap and jerk of my roommate's curtain as he
draws it open

to look and look at my singing mother and her silent choir

and to wink at me with an understanding that passeth peace, this
kind, skeletal man

suffering from end-stage heart disease who loves science fiction
and okra,

who on my first night here read aloud his grandson's bar mitzvah
speech to me,

". . . In my haftorah portion, the Lord takes Ezekiel to a valley full
of bones,

the Lord commands him to prophesy over the bones so they will
become people . . . ,"

and solemnly recited the entire text of the candlelighting ceremony,

"I would like to light the first candle in memory of Grandma Ruth,
   for whom I was named,

I would like Grandma Dot and Grandpa Dan to come up and light
   the second candle,

I would like Aunt Mary Ann and my Albuquerque cousins Alanna
   and Susanna to come up and light the third candle . . . ,"

his voice rising steadily through the vinegary smell and brutal hush
   in the room,

may the Lord hear our listening, His word like matchlight cupped to
   a cigarette

the instant before the intake of breath, like the smoke clouds pooled
   in the lit tobacco

before flooding the lungs and bloodstream, filtering into pith
   and marrow,

may He see Himself again in the hemophiliac's motorcycle

on a certain Sunday in 1975—Hidden Hills Raceway, Gallipolis, Ohio,

a first moto holeshot and wire-to-wire win, a miraculously benign
   sideswipe early on in the second moto

bending the handlebars and front brake lever before the possessed
   rocketing up through the pack

to finish third after passing Brian Kloser on his tricked-out
    Suzuki RM125

midair over the grandstand double jump—

may His absence arrive like that again here in this hygienic room,

not with the rush of a peaked power band and big air over the jumps

but with the strange intuitive calm of that race, a stillness
    somehow poised

in the body even as it pounded and blasted and held its line across
    the washboard track,

may His silence plague us like that again,

may He bless our listening and our homely tongues.

ii

· · · · · ·

At Burt Lake

· · · · · ·

To disappear into the right words
and to be their meanings . . .

October dusk.
Pink scraps of clouds, a plum-colored sky.
The sycamore tree spills a few leaves.
The cold focuses like a lens . . .

Now night falls, its hair
caught in the lake's eye.

Such clarity of things. Already
I've said too much . . .

                    Lord,
language must happen to you
the way this black pane of water,
chipped and blistered with stars,
happens to me.

Ars Poetica

. . . . . .

The dead drag a grappling hook for the living.
The hook is enormous. Suddenly it is tiny.
Suddenly one's voice is a small body falling
through silt and weeds, reaching wildly . . .

Praying with George Herbert in Late Winter

1

In fits and starts, Lord,
   our words work
the other side of language

where you lie if you can be said
   to lie. Mercy upon
the priest who calls on you

to nurture and to terrorize
   him, for you oblige.
Mercy upon you, breath's engine

returning what is to what is.
   Outside, light swarms
and particularizes the snow;

tree limbs crack with ice
   and drop. I can say
there is a larger something

inside me. I can say,
   "Gratitude is
a strange country." But what

would I give to live there?

2

Something breaks in us,
and keeps breaking. Charity,
be severe with me.
Mercy, lay on your hands.

White robes on
the cypress tree. Sparrows
clot the fence posts;
they hop once and weave

through the bleached air.
Lord, I drift on the words
I speak to you—
the words take on

and utter me. In what
language are you not
what *we* say you are?
Surprise me, Lord, as a seed

surprises itself . . .

3

Today the sun has the inward look
of the eye of the Christ Child.
    Grace falls at odd angles from heaven

    to earth: my sins are bright sparks
in the dark of blamelessness . . .
    Yes. From my window I watch a boy step

    backwards down the snow-covered road,
studying his sudden boot tracks.
    The wedding of his look and the world!

    And for a moment, Lord, I think
I understand about you and silence . . .
    But what a racket I make in telling you.

A Visit to the Cathedral

. . . . . .

After the sudden hush and cool
as the doors close,

after we inch into the north aisle
as though into a held breath,

after we cluster like bees around
the jeweled splinter of the True Cross,

I see another nave envelop the nave,
immense, borne up

by the buttresses and cross-ribbed vaults
of what you said to me just now.

Reading Frank O'Hara in the Hospital

· · · · · ·

1

The IV drips its slow news.
So long, lean and turbulent morning!
I wonder if my roommate would swap

2

Schlegel's *Lucinde* for his scrambled eggs?
Each thing bears its gifts,
the power lines' birds settle and cry out:

3

"You too could be Premier of France,
if only . . .
if only . . ."

4

The lights
in here are so excitement prone!
but the sun is undefended. Doctor,

5

I feel like I'm rushing
toward you with an olive branch . . .
With my cheese sandwich and wrist tag,

6

I could be six years old again—
look out, jungle gym! Now
outside I hear "a bulldozer in heat

7

stuck in mud." And the world
narrows to this window above
the hospital gift shop. No, it widens.

Reading the Tao Te Ching in the Hospital

. . . . . .

The ceiling closes in like an argument
then floats off, losing the thread . . .

The room listens. The room empties
its mind of me. *The more*

you speak of it, the less you understand.

A glass of water. The arrangement
of pills in a paper cup. The precise
folds of the pillowcase—

substantial as fear
or need. *Hold on to the center.*

To speak one word bright
with attention. To wait and wake
perpetually to the room's

anonymous plunge.

When Comfort Arrives

· · · · · ·

1

Are there comings and goings among the stars?
Who would look for signs this evening,

when the sky seems wrong from your small room
and the future appears as something forgotten?

You want to walk and keep walking,
tense steps toward an early home . . .

You think the crickets, the moonlight, are better
than you. When comfort arrives, how will you see it,

by what dark luggage? Your friends know.
Its speech, they say, is a listening;

its mercy is severe—
empty yourself, and again.

2

A selfless song is its own praise.
Mandelstam said that. Moments of splendor

seen from the other side of a chained door.
Goldfinch, lilac, pine forest. The spiderweb

of light. Death is no terrible height
you peer over now and then—

it's simple, a fine silence, rain on black
earth. You almost see him, waving his arms

in a blizzard and disappearing.
I want to give back this dust

I've borrowed, he wrote once. And later,
It's no longer me singing, it's my breath.

3

You're walking, disappearing into a stand of elms
at evening, the way thought disappears before sleep,

or the way your voice disappears and you hear,
suddenly, another's voice, blaming you . . .

The nonsense of crickets. The moon bleaches
the grass, the elms swell as a low wind lifts.

You want to know what your hands know,
gripping a cattail, picking a ripe pear.

Or what your breath knows, its rise and fall
a slow, steady song. It's late. Somewhere

your friends imagine the worst about you.
In fear for you, and in something like love.

4

The sky pitches its blue tent. A crisp day.
You wonder if you aren't here to interpret:

the smell of thyme in a neighbor's garden,
the wind with its gift of a strange tongue.

Cows graze on a hillside. They're not
overlooking you. Still, there is

always a bitter ache holding you back
from the pure joy of giving up. Always

a reason to seek God's lucid ear.
You watch a spider assemble the air

and a cardinal lifts from a branch in flame.
Sometimes you look for the world, and it's there.

5

The dead are articulate, and know what to say.
The dead are not destroyers.

So many stories clamoring for attention,
asking to be yours . . .

You think of Mandelstam, of the determined script
of the letters of your friends. Imagination

as bridge. On the other side of
understanding, a goldfinch is providing.

A time comes when you want to account for tears
and wrong silences, when the promises

you make to yourself
and to others are the same promises . . .

6

You're walking again, this time with a friend.
—Both of you curious, both of you

tongue-tied under the sure drift of the stars.
You're learning the patience it takes to stride

in time with another. You want to pull a few words
from your life, speak to this listening face:

Most everything I know doesn't matter.
The night sky is as brilliant as the day sky,

you think, a vast, black astonishment . . .
Most, your friend says. *You're here now. Are you cold?*

The wind. The thread of quiet. You want
what your friend wants. A careful, human voice.

7

We're always looking for some good advice,
and anyone who will listen to it.

Stand up and feel your stiff body steady itself.
Step from the porch and watch the light blow all over you.

Once, you left despair at a friend's door
like a child to be looked after.

Your friend said, *Tomorrow your life will matter
to us both.* You laughed, and slept.

There is no word for the stark gratitude
we feel for friends. Just more advice:

Take your own pulse once in a while.
Consider the ant, and be wise.

8

Driving to Petoskey, you pass struck raccoons,
avenues of pines, miles of stripped birch trees

rising like broken pencils from the hills
and thawing marshes. A red-tailed hawk hangs

like a speck of black soot in the rearview mirror.
This far north, summer inches up through the earth

like spring. You're learning the trick of the good
daydream: the quieting words, sure images

of failure trailed by possible love. Yes,
leave comfort root-room, and try to name it.—

The word you want to say is a little word,
just big enough for the sweat bee, the inchworm . . .

9

Vulture and star, hyacinth and sun. The patient
hats of Queen Anne's lace. Say everything,

everything witnesses. The tide edits the shore-
line and the first light primes the sky; say

morning invites your small talk. *Dew slips from
a fern. It will rain. Where are the trilliums?*

Here is a story. The sky hums, some dragonflies
pause over their shadows and dart off.

An awkward moment comes when you say, *This is
my life.* Earnestly, without regret. The trilliums

are gone, the tiny veins of new ferns fill with rain.
There is no substitute for a lifetime.

Evening Song

· · · · · ·

The crickets go on with their shrill music.
The sun drops down.

What was it my brother said to me once
in Charleston, before he disappeared that spring
like the quick wake of a water mite?

This was 1980, evening, the porch lights burning.
He was reading from *The Cloud of Unknowing*.

Robins gossiped in the poplars,
moths spiraled across the uncut grass.
Moonlight wormed through the neighboring lawns.

We must therefore pray . . . not in many words,
but in a little word of one syllable.

Didn't he say forgiveness was his homely double?
Didn't he say what I wanted him to say? Maybe
I wasn't listening, chewing a branch of sassafras . . .

But I doubt it. As I doubt, now, that the life
of my lawn is a still life, the moon and shrill chants

opinions on despair. There are times
when the sound the world makes is a little word.
Something like *help*, or *yes* . . .

iii

Hymning the Kanawha

. . . . . .

1

>   Day brings a steady
> hand, a sure breath every other day . . .

My brother again on the edge of his bed,
sitting up with his eyes closed,
his palms pressed, a brief prayer.

>   *You see we're in trouble*

Spring, 1972. The last flare
of an April dusk. Sure breaths and relief
after a run on dialysis. He's telling
an old story, his slim translations
of Psalms, to whoever is listening.

>   *Give us strength enough*

The passionate calm after a run—
his pulse grows as the fresh blood thins,
his drugged face opens like a fist.

>   *

Runnels of spring rain. Branches
like floating ribs from the camphor trees.

Someone is asking you to make a fist.
Someone is taking your pulse
and saying nothing, and starting to weep

over the jonquils and the yellow grass,
over the cold surge of the Kanawha River.

2

Slurs on the Psalms he calls these prayers.
And writes them out
in a notebook he keeps under his pillow,
and shows no one.

> *Death has fallen on me*
> *like a stone I can't budge*
>
> *Once death was my companion*
> *We walked together in your house*

It's an odd-numbered day,
the machine, like another child, bathed and asleep.

Before he sleeps tonight, my brother will forgive
his body anything—night sores, bad numbers,
pain like a word . . .

Before sleep, my brother will bless himself, and lie down.

*

The blood in a black widow falls asleep.

Near an almond branch,
work ants gather their meals in the noon sun.

At the far edge of a field, a hospital
is erected and torn down
on the same day, the healers now

working double time, now obsolete,
your failed kidneys swelling from pinholes

to buttonholes, buttonholes to large red sacks.

3

What's in the doctor's pause and the heart's,
the needle placed like a root
in the red vein . . .

The machine drones through the afternoon.
My parents shuffle about him, keeping the lines clean,
smoothing the blood's slow run from the body.

> But I am no one
> I am poured out like water

Scissor-clamps, the pump, coils: the hours
are counted out. Like coins, like yesterday's
good news, they pile up
just out of reach.

> Lord, be near

*

X rays of the hip joint, fat negatives,
milk-light your wronged bones.
For once you can hear yourself:

Syringe of sleep,
Syringe of another life,
close my eyes,
lift these white walls.

Your shadow ascends like a soul
from the stretcher but holds still.
In time, in good time, your own blood

mutters and wakes.

4

"Just to imagine
there is something larger than me, and purer."

Thus my brother, in a notebook, 1972.
A reason to rise in the long mornings.
Thus sun, moon, ghost-of-a-chance; what
the Psalms say.

> How long will sorrow flow
> through my heart like bad blood
> How long will you be a stranger
>
> Like anyone
> I'm dying

He writes at his desk, sure breath after
sure breath. Outside, the poplars; and I'm
spinning a ball through a netted hoop

over and over, getting better.

    *

Reedstem, cattail, eyelash, a leaf . . .
A fine rain peppers the Kanawha, a cold
wind hustles the yew bushes and hollyhocks
in Tuendiewei Park. The log cabin there

rests on your fingertip, twilit; inside,
your grandparents parade in your white gowns,
their eyes the color of your eyes, their wake
the dust prints you'll leave behind.

5

There's a photograph, a boy on a beach, 1961.
My father took it. My brother
didn't know it. He sat on the hot sands,
tracing his noon shadow with a Lego stick.

Heat came in with the waves. He was five.
Morning opened up
like a torn fingernail, and began to bleed.
Eleven years. He sits under himself now, the flush
and pull of dialysis; writing sentences.

> *The river of God is full*
> *of water*

The edge of his straw hat casts a shadow
like gray fingers, water reeds. Gulls
tattooed the beach. At five, my brother saw

his shadow as a circle. Widening, opening.

*

The hallway goes out like a blown
candle, and you're back at your first house—

flies in the screen's light, white wings
fluttering through the grilled blackness.

You walk toward the coal cars by the riverbank:
damp smell of the cornfield at night;

over your head, the same stars
in their ordered slide . . .

Only this time it's wrong,
the face of the night nurse among the reeds

and birch branches, the whole landscape
caught like a moth in the renal room's dark.

6

Tonight, asleep, my brother walks
out into a mild rain on the driveway.
The pulse, he'll say, of drops collecting
into puddles is his pulse, the soft tick
against the windows his tick . . .

And tomorrow's an odd-numbered day,
nothing but sleep and a book.

> *a little sleep, a little folding*
> *of the hands*

My father goes out to bring him back
inside. He knows that he will keep this:
his son asleep in his pale flesh,

part of this rain and the black sky,
part of these black puddles filling the potholes
in the driveway.
                    (The hands ghostly, so steady . . .)

My brother is led to a dry bed, and lies down
whispering after a rain, the quiet
before a sleepwalker's footsteps . . .

           *

Your family, gathering themselves forever.

They play cards, or read, and wait for your step
and your suit of scars.
They stare past one another into

the river, and go on
waiting until your voice fills
the breezes again, until

the shine of the Kanawha
becomes their shine.

7

The machine drones like an old complaint.
My brother's shunt—a tubed sleeve, blood-vines
scaling the entire room, a red trellis
of veins. I'm eleven and looking on
for hours, as though over a roof's edge.

> *The peace of a good family*
> *like rare oil*
> *like your name*

We try to talk. Already, I know
the wrong words to say. I've rehearsed
the gestures of my hands, how fear
enters a child's voice. He's telling me
that it's all right, that if the mind
is lucid it can shine
like blown glass in a brilliant light . . .

His hands shake. His drugged face
blurs like a moon.

*

You sit in a silence of rivers, the last
April driftings of the Kanawha, and watch
your own ashes being raised in wind

and scattered on the bank. Your family
looks on without a word. In a dry cove,
they've waited for your body to float by

like driftwood, for your one call
from the nettles, from the crickets' chirrs,
from the flash of fireflies low in the grass . . .

8

When God died my brother learned to sing.
When God died my brother slipped through the house
like wind, rustling his papers and spread sheets
before leaving under a door without a sound.

> *Lord, I look at the night sky*
> *and see your fingerprints*

> *What are we, almost you*
> *There's sheep oxen birds*
> *There's the sea there's the field*

> *through which we see your vital hands*

Scissor-clamps, the pump, coils. The hours
are counted out. But a sure breath fills
the planet, and another—what the Psalms say—

a sure breath, a steady hand, every other day.

*

Along the east bank of the Kanawha River,
your shadow swells to its own poise

and walks into the chigger bush, burrs
clinging like tiny scabs to the silhouette.

It finds the warm grass in Tuendiewei Park
and lies down. It considers your guilt

and lies down. It turns back to the Kanawha
and rises, and slides into the black water,

your body drifting across the white
bedsheets, a slow erasure of your name . . .

Codeine Diary

. . . . . .

On November 15, 1972—one week after Nixon was reelected—I clapped my hands for fourteen hours and thirty-one minutes. I was listed in *The Guinness Book of World Records*. I was eleven years old.

My record was published on page 449 of the 1974 edition of the *Guinness Book*, landlocked between the listings for "Largest Circus" and "Club Swinging," in the chapter entitled "Human Achievements":

> *Clapping*. The duration record for continuous clapping is 14 hours 31 minutes by Thomas C. Andrews (b. April 30, 1961) at Charleston, West Virginia on November 15, 1972. He sustained an average of 120 claps per minute and an audibility range of at least 100 yards.

*

I would like to feel a stirring in my knee, calf, and ankle: a signal that the blood pooled there is being absorbed at last and the joints are opening again, like a fist or a jonquil.

*

I make $12,500 a year. I work as a copy editor for *Mathematical Reviews*, a bibliographic journal for mathematicians, physicists, statisticians, logicians, historians and philosophers of mathematics. When Joyce said he wrote for an ideal reader suffering from an ideal insomnia, he might well have had our subscribers in mind. At least they seem to be up all night, reading, assaying, scribbling after absolutes in a language the clipped densities of which rival, on a good night, any passage from *Finnegans Wake*.

*

I would like to feel a stirring.

*

Today is Thursday.

*

I'm writing this from my bed at the University of Michigan Hospital. It is 3 a.m. It is the half-dark of hospitals at night. I have had an accident. I have been in an accident.

From my window I can make out the iced-over Huron River and a tennis court covered with a taut white sheet of snow.

*

Philadelphia Enquirer November 28, 1972
Martin Bormann Reported Alive in South America
Champions' Routes to Glory
. . . And sometimes champions have highly developed imaginations that help them in their quest for glory. Tom Andrews, only 11, of Charleston, W.Va., applauded without interruption for 14 hours 31 minutes. His father, Ray, so attested in an affidavit he sent to *The Guinness Book of World Records*.

The National Tattler January 28, 1973
Boy Breaks Hand-Clapping Record
He Probably Never Will Applaud Anyone!

Dear Tom,

It was certainly nice to read that you have broken the world's record in clapping. Keep your Dad busy getting that affidavit recorded.

We used to enjoy seeing how your Dad recorded you and John in your annual picture for Christmas. The last few years we had lost contact.

Congratulations again. Everyone is very proud of you.

Sincerely,

The Ripley Fishers

National Enquirer September 9, 1973
Director Who Made 'South Pacific' Reveals He Was Mentally Ill for 28 Years
Twins Engaged, Married and Have Babies on Same Day
Smothering Sneezes Can Harm You, Warns Doctor
11-Year-Old Boy Claps 94,520 Times in 14 Hours 31 Minutes
Tom Andrews doesn't expect anybody to give him a hand for breaking a world record. Especially after clapping for himself an astounding 94,520 times!

"I just wanted to break a world record," grinned freckle-faced Tom, who lives with his parents in Charleston, W.Va.

Norris McWhirter, co-compiler of the *Guinness Book*, told the *Enquirer*: "We don't have many 11-year-olds in the *Guinness Book*. So this is quite a remarkable feat."

Dear Tom,

Try to come out if you can, but if you can't that's o.k. I can play till about 4:00 or 5:00. I hope you come out. Will you walk with me today? Circle   YES   NO

I think you are the nicest boy over in Rolling Hills. I'm going to try to get you something.

Love, Diane

P.S. Write back if you want to. Don't let anybody else see this except Nan if you want to. Or Laura. I just showed Nan and Laura. Do you mind? Circle   YES   NO

Answer questions and give back, please.

*

"That your scrapbook?" Ellen, the night nurse, asks.

When I mutter that, technically, it's my mother's, who brought it to the hospital to cheer me up, Ellen glances at the *National Enquirer* headline and says, "You did that? Clapped your hands?"

I nod.

"Lord!" she says. "Did you have a major bleed, or what?"

*

Two days after my brother died I learned to juggle apples.

As children John and I stared in wonder at jugglers, at the blurred orbits of their hovering knives or bowling pins, at their taunting nonchalance. Gravity flowed from their fingers. Two days after John died, in Charleston for the funeral, I traced on notebook paper the looping flight paths three objects must follow to remain aloft while being shuttled from hand to hand. I was staying at my great-aunt's apartment on Kanawha Boulevard. She kept a bowl of fresh fruit on a coffee table in the living room, where I found three apples of serviceable size and with them made an inelegant leap from theory to practice. I kept dropping the same apple. Once it fell against a corner of the coffee table: the yellow skin split and juice began to drip. I dropped it again. More juice. And again. The smell was terrific, sweet as just-washed hair. Eventually I could keep all three bruised, dripping apples weaving in midair, circulating. Gravity flowed from my fingers.

*

I have had an accident.

*

I have had an accident on the sidewalk. I watched my feet come out from under me on the iced concrete with a kind of anecdotal perspective. The bleeding inside the joints, the infusions of factor VIII, the weeks of immobility, the waiting for codeine, the inventions with which my mind would veer in the direction of solid ground— as my weight drilled into the twisting leg I saw the whole pantomime emerge with the clarity of blown glass.

*

Sunrise. The sky gray and pink.

*

My roommate, an elderly man with end-stage heart disease, was rolled in on a stretcher today. Oxygen tubes curl around his ears, line his cheek, enter his nostrils. His wife reads newspapers while he sleeps. They look uncannily alike: white-haired, slight, their salmon-colored faces stretched tightly across the facial bones. He's yet to be awake in this room.

*

When I told my hematologist that as a teenager I had raced motocross, that in fact in one race in Gallipolis, Ohio, I had gotten the holeshot and was bumped in the first turn and run over by twenty-some motorcycles, she said, "No. Not with your factor level. I'm sorry, but you wouldn't withstand the head injuries. You like the sound of yourself being dramatic."

*

The riffled sea of my sheets.

*

There is a mathematical process, useful to physicists and probability theorists, called the "self-avoiding random walk." Walter, one of MR's physics editors, once explained it to me as a succession of movements along a lattice of given dimensions, where the direction and length of each move is randomly determined, and where the walk does not return to a point already walked on. I almost wept with delight.

Walter looked confused. "You studied randomness in school?" he said, earnestly.

*

So many infusions of factor VIII . . .

As the concentrate filters into the IV drip, I feel the cold rise up through the upper arm, the shoulder, then branch off descending into the chest. I contain multitudes.

*

Heels clicking by in the hallway.

*

Later I learned that Walter would sometimes perform a kind of mime when he was drunk, a bodily interpretation of the self-avoiding random walk. Walter wore wire-rim glasses and a long, dazzlingly unkempt beard. He had close friends everywhere: Kyoto, Glasgow, Milan, Leningrad, Sao Paulo, Cape Town. I tried to imagine his self-avoidance. Head crooked severely, eyes fixed, doll-like, in the opposite direction, feet turned alternately inward and outward, arms flailing somehow along trajectories his head, eyes, and feet did not intersect. I liked Walter. He refused to publish a review of any paper that referred to "cone-shaped objects" and their velocity, heat-seeking ability, etc.

*

In the hallway in the shunt-light
of the hallway
you wake
a nurse comes to show you
to your room
but can't find it
the entire wing is missing
you look outside
there in the gravel lot the sleet
pounding its fists
your white gown is walking home

    *

Ellen takes the ice pack off my right calf and feels for a pulse at the
ankle. She's been doing this every five minutes throughout the night
to make sure the pressure of bleeding hasn't compressed and finally
flattened the blood vessels. I'm a half hour or so into a dose of
codeine: removing the ice pack doesn't make me cry out.

    "It's still so hot," she says, meaning the skin around the calf. "You
could fry an egg on it."

    *

Glaring light. Shocking cold of the bedpan.

    *

The President through the TV's drift and snow: "Things are even more like they are now than they've ever been."

    *

Body positioning, weight distribution, throttle control.
    Work with the bike. Don't fight it.
    The sooner you shift your weight out of a corner, the sooner you can accelerate. Don't lose time between braking and accelerating.
    Use the bike's ability to control itself.
    Preparing the bike—the gear ratios, the suspension, the jetting—ahead of time will help your ability to concentrate on the race.
    Concentration: don't let something stupid happen in the lulling middle of a race.
    Adapt to the track as it changes. Be on the lookout for alternative lines.
    Racing in the rain: controlled insanity. Get out front to avoid being roosted with mud from the rear tires of other riders.

    *

There are times, in the last minutes before I am allowed, or allow myself, more codeine, when the pain inside the joints simplifies me utterly. I feel myself descending some kind of evolutionary ladder until I become as crude and guileless as an amoeba. The pain is not personal. I am incidental to it. It is like faith, the believer eclipsed by something immense . . .

    *

You like the sound of yourself being dramatic.

     *

Carrie's with me, often, during the day.

Her face. Her being here.

Our talks, and long easy silences.

     *

"Does he have to do that?" the waitress at Pizza Hut asked. She passed out glasses of ice water from a tray, then set the tray down on the table.

"He's breaking a world record," John said flatly.

"Does it bother you?" my mother said. "I can't make him stop, but we can leave."

The waitress looked up. "You're joking, right? Let me see." She gestured for me to pull my hands out from under the table.

I showed my hands. Eyes, hostile, were staring from neighboring booths and tables.

"He has to sustain an audibility range of at least one hundred yards," John said.

"I'm getting the cook," she said. "He's got to see this."

A minute later a thin man with botched teeth, wearing a blue dough-smeared apron, was glaring at me. "Well," he said impatiently, "let's see your deal."

Again I showed my hands. I speeded up, just a little, the rate of clapping.

"Right. Unbelievable," the cook said, shaking his head and disappearing. I said, "Can we order?"

"What do you do if you have to go to the bathroom?" the waitress asked.

"I'd like a root beer," I said. "Do you have root beer?"

"He's trying to go the whole day without going," my mother said.

"Good luck!" the waitress said.

I said, "Do you have root beer?"

"Yeah, they have root beer," John said.

I said, "I was asking her, thank you very much."

"I don't think I could go the whole day," the waitress said. "I think I have a weak bladder."

I leaned over to John and whispered: "Help."

"Hey," said the waitress, "how are you going to eat pizza?"

"I'm not," I said. "I'm just sipping some root beer. If you have it."

"They have it, they have it," John said.

John buried his head in his hands.

"I'm going to feed him," my mother said.

"No way!" I said.

For a second I forgot to clap, then caught myself and reestablished my rhythm.

"We'll have a large mushroom and pepperoni," my mother said. "And I'd like a glass of iced tea. What do you want to drink?"

"I want a coke," John said.

"Root beer," I said.

*

Night. Snow falling past the window. It is codeine, breaking up and falling softly over the small field and train tracks, over the plowed roads, over the houses and apartment buildings, the river, the tall trees furred with ice.

*

When I was falling in love with Carrie, I wanted to astonish her with some simple devastating gesture, like the harmonica line in Neil Young's "Heart of Gold."

*

My roommate's lungs labor through sleep, each breath a furrow plowed in earth.

*

After the waitress left, my mother lectured me about not participating in events we scheduled on John's "off-days"—days when he wasn't on the dialysis machine. "You've known for a week that we were coming here. You could have picked another day for this clapping business." She said this in front of John, who grimaced and began looking around the room.

My argument was that just being there at Pizza Hut, while I was in the crucial early hours of breaking a world record, was sufficient participation, and that sipping a little root beer, under the circumstances, put me solidly in the off-day spirit of things.

She didn't see it that way.

I asked John what he thought. He shook his head; he wanted
nothing to do with this conversation.

I kept clapping under the table. Later, after the waitress asked,
giggling, if everything was all right with our pizza, I let my mother
feed me a bite or two.

*

The sound of a dog barking ferociously.

*

There is a sleep like the long dissolve
of bone into brown dirt. The nurse carries
a paper cup, a syringe of that sleep . . .

But the chrysanthemums, and the trees outside
the window, say: *You are never tired enough.*

My second breath says it, and the room's tick,
the star-tiled floor, the chalk walls
through the night hours. I lie listening

as though to a voice inside my voice, a lullaby
deep in the throat. Now a small snowfall.
Now a first blur of sun staining the window.

*

Listening to Carrie's Walkman. A radio play from the fifties.

"Hey, how'd you like a nice cool tall glass of water, chock-full of ice?"

"Sounds great."

"Well you're not going to get it you murderer!"

*

Dawn. Sunlight in defined rays through the clouds like spokes of a great wheel. There is a phrase for it. Yes. Sun dog.

*

I was elected to Phi Beta Kappa, graduated *summa cum laude* in philosophy, and went to work at 7-11. This was in 1984. I wasn't terribly well qualified, but I had worked at Sears when I was in high school and the manager needed a body behind the cash register pronto. So I got the job. When the matter of my hemophilia came up, the manager shrugged and said, "You shouldn't have any trouble. Unless somebody knocks you out or something."

I asked how often that was likely to happen.

"Hardly ever. Two months ago on the midnight shift a guy bashed my face in with a pistol butt. But that's really rare. If a guy holds you up, Southland wants you to give up the money. Don't be a hero. But since we just got hit up the odds are it won't happen again for, oh, eight months or so. It's the cycle of things."

*

Günter Eich wrote that "in each good line of poetry I hear the cane of the blindman striking: I am on secure ground now." Good or bad, each sentence I get down before the codeine wears off is a toehold toward equilibrium. Each phrase, quotation, memory, self-avoiding or not.

*

John, you're vague as mist, dressed up in dew, smoke. I keep seeing you, haunting the hawthorn trees within earshot of the riverbank. Asking nothing.

*

On Election Day I called my hematologist.

"Fourteen hours of clapping," she said, "could provoke a bleed in the palms, the wrists, in the muscles of the forearms . . ."

*

The days are perceptibly longer, lighter.

*

My leg shimmers, spreading its colors like a peacock: cinnabar, copper, rust, olive, ruddle, gentian, umber . . .

*

Brother, I always compare you
to a drifting log with iron nails in it
You float ashore   I pick you out on the beach
I'm building a small house with you

I always compare you to the sun
when the earth grows dark awhile
passing behind the clouds

     *

I can see my heart beat through my hospital gown.

     *

What surprised me was how easy it was to keep a precise and
consistent rhythm. Two hours into the record, I felt as if my hands,
like the legs of runners who have broken through the "wall," could
hammer away at themselves effortlessly and indefinitely. At that point
I knew I would not start a bleed. I had no doubt. And yet my hands
kept hammering at themselves. Hammering.

     *

Sometimes my roommate's breathing speeds up suddenly, like quick
deep hits on a cigarette. This lasts only a few seconds.

     *

"Nixon's problem is, he's not eating right," my mother said. "It's
plain as day, anyone can see it. Just look at the man."

It was 5:30 p.m. and I was still at it, 120 claps per minute.

"Care for a drink?" my father said to himself. "Don't mind if I do, thank you for asking."

*

This morning I missed the plastic urinal, fouling the sheets.

*

The knee is locked at a forty-five–degree angle. Blood rushed the joint's interior, filled it, kept rushing. The muscles are shrinking to the shape of the bent leg.

"Straighten it as far as you comfortably can," says my hematologist. "But don't push it. What we want to avoid is another bleed inside the joint."

Yes. Yes.

*

A creekbed some goldenrod the tall
grasses arcing
over the flat field
you're walking a thin dirt path
the creek the faint rush of water
you watch your breath rise
like woodsmoke in first light

as a sudden memory
of ice across flesh returns the night
nurse saying *good morning*

    *

Outside, snow's falling again. The loyal and fragmented snow.

    *

This bed as embryonic world. Its vast cerulean distances, its
equatorial thickets. Regions of hissing ash, monsoons, midnight
suns. To move my leg a few inches: an emigration from Tashkent to
Bogotá. To turn over: an impossible odyssey, a tale for Jules Verne.

    *

Carrie tells me about a snowman children have built near our
apartment. It's wearing Ray-Ban sunglasses and stereo headphones. I
imagine the children at work on the torso. Snowball fights. Circling
footprints. Their serious expressions, as if they'd just been reading
the *Critique of Pure Reason*. The breath from their curses pluming in air.

    *

She comes and goes, my hematologist. Sometimes a half dozen
interns cluster around her. They look like children, rich white
kids playing doctor, stethoscopes dangling absurdly from their
gleaming necks.

    *

Glancing through a galley set from MR, I find a paper—"Specification of an Algorithm for the Economizing of Memory"—with this: "An associative memory can be defined as a transformation between two sets. . . . This associative memory is shown to converge rapidly, and to have noise rejection properties and some learning capability."

*

Here, now

A pressure, a packed-in rawness in my back. Like a boot heel pressing down hard, but from inside the tissue out.

I'm pushing a hole through the buzzer to Ellen. A bruise in my thumb is nothing.

*

Hours in codeine's loose grip.

*

In the parking lot outside Pizza Hut John stepped on the heel of my shoe. My heel popped out. "Flat tire?" John said.

I tried to slide back into my shoe without using my hands, which clapped and clapped.

"Knock knock," John said.

"Who's there," I said.

My mother held the door to Pizza Hut open for us.

"Tom," he said.

"Forget it," I said. "Nothing doing."

*

X rays: thick smears of charcoal. I've bled into the muscles along the spinal column. "If the bleeding becomes intraspinal," my hematologist says, "paralysis is a not unlikely scenario." What can we do? "We can maintain," she says, "a factor VIII level of 40 to 50 percent for ten to fourteen days."

*

I turn my name over in my hand;
dull sleeve I slide in and out of.

*

For a long time I asked John to come watch me race. Again and again he refused. Finally he agreed to come to a race at Hidden Hills Raceway in Gallipolis, Ohio—to shut me up, I think, as much as to satisfy his curiosity about his hemophiliac brother racing a motorcycle across the gouged wilderness.

The road from Charleston to Gallipolis follows the Kanawha River to Point Pleasant, where the Kanawha and the Ohio rivers converge in a vast capital T sunk into bottomland. We passed coal barges drudging through the black water, their wakes spreading across the width of the river and lapping both banks. Before we got to Point Pleasant a heavy rain started. Past Gallipolis, just past the farms and headquarters of Bob Evans Restaurants, we turned off the interstate onto a series of rain-slicked fire-roads that led to the track. We were hauling: three times the pickup nearly slid off the road's shoulder. Eventually we pulled into the pit area at Hidden Hills. I wondered what John made of the scene. Riders tooling the pits with their helmets and shirts off, sideburned, thick arms tattooed and flexing. The smell of Bel-Ray oil and WD40. The ribbon of track snaking the Ohio landscape. Someone gunning a bike's motor; its spit and cough before going silent. He said nothing.

I knew John would have to wear a plastic bag over his shunt arm to keep the dust out. We were lucky it rained. Dust usually billowed wildly after the start of a race, a huge rolling wave breaking over the hills and shrouding the spectators. Rain would keep the dirt moist and on the track.

Midway through the practice sessions, however, the rain stopped. By the time of the first 125 moto, dust forced John into the cab of the pickup.

That is the image that attacks me now. John in the truck, windows rolled up, reading a book to pass the time while I kicked up the dust all around him.

*

An endless surge and drip of facts from the TV . . .

Israel is the most successful nation in the world in increasing rainfall artificially . . .

One billion years ago the sun was 20 to 30 percent dimmer . . .

Donald Duck received 291 votes in the Swedish election for prime minister . . .

Hang gliders in Los Angeles are using their bird's-eye view to help local police and fire departments . . .

*

This fierce inward stalking of patience.

*

I can feel the spinal muscles harden, filling with blood. I cannot straighten my back. The skin is boiling, sharp dots of heat along the spine like water in a pan. Or, alternately, an even heat just under the skin's surface, a steady flaming intensity.

*

"You have to imagine Richard Nixon as a little boy," my mother said. "A boy with a mother and a father, just like everybody else."
   Now I tried to muffle the sound of my clapping.
   "It's not that simple," my father said, "and you know it."

*

Carrie holding watch over me. Sadness visible in the folds of her wrinkled clothes.

*

In this morning's dream I was a clarinetist, giving a concert at DeVos Hall in Grand Rapids, soloing in a piece titled "Concerto for Clarinet and Cheese." It was poorly attended. At a certain point in the performance, the sound of my clarinet began to dwindle, as if a microphone were being turned down slowly. The baffled conductor stopped the orchestra. I played on. One could barely hear the melody by now, but the sound of the clarinet valves clicking open and shut was rising inexplicably through the concert hall, becoming a simultaneous music, underneath or alongside the blown notes, feeding them with staccato percussion. In this way the melody, slowly restored, and the clicking of the valves met as equals in the performance . . .

*

I can't shut out the sound of my roommate's breathing.

*

This morning my banana had a "Cholesterol Free" sticker on it.

*

Nine a.m. My mother and father arrive, emissaries from the mysterious sunlit world.

*

Random symmetries . . . Days when John's shunt clotted and he required I forget how many cc's of heparin to get his blood to stop coagulating.

Meanwhile, I'd start a bleed, and would need cryoprecipitate or factor VIII to get my blood to clot . . .

*

Tomorrow's forecast: "Just clouds."

*

More X rays. I've stopped bleeding into the spinal muscles. Soon
enough, my hematologist says, my body will loosen and break down
and absorb the hardened blood surrounding the spine, as it has been
doing in my leg. There has been no intraspinal bleeding, no bleeding
into the kidney or liver.

I look at Carrie. I look at my mother and father. We are inside a
sudden astonishing calm. I seem to levitate and hover over the white
sheets . . .

*

Once when John was dialyzing I tripped into the machine and jerked
a tube clean out of its socket. John's blood pumped and sprayed into
the air, splattering across the carpet and splotching our skin and
clothes. My mother worked frantically to reconnect the tube and to
stabilize John's blood pressure.

Later I noticed that some of the blood had seeped inside a picture
frame on the wall beside the dialysis chair. The frame held a
photograph of John and me wading in the Kanawha River, staring
hard at the gray water.

*

Walking. Dew clings to the bunch grass.
The IV pushes a ghost needle back
into the vein. As I touch the bruises,

my eyes find work in the early sunlight,
my feet find their prints in the field.

Notes

• • • • • •

"The Hemophiliac's Motorcycle": The lines quoting haftorah and candle-lighting ceremony speeches were written by Ronald Kimball on the occasion of his bar mitzvah in Ann Arbor, Michigan, September 1988.

"When Comfort Arrives": Certain lines have been adapted or simply stolen without acknowledgment from the following. The seventh line of the sixth section is from Jack Ridl's poem, "In the Woods I Startled a Pheasant"; the last line of the seventh section is from Proverbs 6:6; the tenth line of the eighth section is from Hopkins's "My Own Heart Let Me More Have Pity On"; the last line of the poem is from Ezra Pound's 98th Canto. "When Comfort Arrives" is dedicated to Jack and Julie Ridl.

"Codeine Diary": The poem beginning "Brother, I always compare you . . ." is an adaptation of "The Mourning Song of Small-Lake-Underneath," from John R. Swanton's *Tlingit Myths and Texts* (Bureau of American Ethnology, 1909).

The Iowa Poetry Prize Winners

1987
Elton Glaser, *Tropical Depressions*
Michael Pettit, *Cardinal Points*

1988
Bill Knott, *Outremer*
Mary Ruefle, *The Adamant*

1989
Conrad Hilberry, *Sorting the Smoke*
Terese Svoboda, *Laughing Africa*

1993
Tom Andrews, *The Hemophiliac's Motorcycle*
Michael Heffernan, *Love's Answer*
John Wood, *In Primary Light*

The Edwin Ford Piper Poetry Award Winners

1990
Philip Dacey, *Night Shift at the Crucifix Factory*
Lynda Hull, *Star Ledger*

1991
Greg Pape, *Sunflower Facing the Sun*
Walter Pavlich, *Running near the End of the World*

1992
Lola Haskins, *Hunger*
Katherine Soniat, *A Shared Life*